The Union Canal

by

GUTHRIE HUTTON

This Sunday School outing at the turn of the century provides a puzzle for the 1990's. Where is it? The most likely place is Muiravonside, but the bridge has been replaced by a culvert and the trees either cut down or attacked by Dutch Elm disease, (which has ravaged trees all along the canal) so it doesn't look like this any more. The boats could have sailed out from Falkirk. Once past the pretty little Muiravonside church, they would have gone through the bridge, turned at the winding hole (or turning place) and come back for the photograph. Am I right? I wish I knew!

First Published in the United Kingdom, 1993
By Richard Stenlake, 1 Overdale Street, Langside, Glasgow G42 9PZ
Tel: 041 632 2304

ISBN 1-872074-23-5

The Union was never an industrial canal. One of its delights today therefore is an ever changing experience of the countryside. The embankments are open to wind, rain and sunshine and offer splendid views over a wide countryside. The sheltered cuttings are damp, with lush vegetation, stillness and privacy. There is wildlife everywhere, a natural realm in symphisis with the adjoining farmland. Farms prospered from their association with the canal. They sent produce to city markets from little wharves, like the one just beyond this bridge near Broxburn.

INTRODUCTION

Edinburgh could not get enough coal. Glasgow could, from the Monkland coalfields through the Monkland Canal and from pits beside the Forth and Clyde Canal "... it's not by slothfulness and ease that Glasgow's canty ingles breeze ..."; but the embarrassed Capital also had a transport problem. Coal coming by sea from Alloa, Fife and Newcastle was subject to a duty of 3/6d a ton, making it very expensive, while bad roads hampered the hundreds of carts that trundled into Edinburgh every day, with coal from Midlothian. A canal was the only answer.

Four proposals were made in the 1790's for a canal from Edinburgh to the Monklands, but they were too expensive. Interest was revived in 1811 and Hugh Baird, the relatively unknown resident engineer of the Forth and Clyde Canal, was commissioned to prepare a new plan. He proposed a canal from Lothian Road to Falkirk, where locks would join it to the Forth and Clyde Canal. The scheme was bitterly attacked in Edinburgh and Leith, because it would advance the interests of the Forth and Clyde Canal Company and promote the port of Grangemouth at the expense of Leith. Counter proposals for a canal starting in Leith were prepared by Robert Stevenson (grandfather of Robert Louis) but failed to attract the necessary backing. Baird's scheme however received support from the great Scottish engineer Thomas Telford who described it as "... the most perfect inland navigation between Edinburgh and Glasgow ...". The doubters were won over and The Edinburgh and Glasgow Union Canal (to give it its full name) was approved by Parliament. The talking was over.

Cutting (you don't build a canal, you 'cut' it) began in March 1818 and continued day and night. It was completed by May 1822 when a boat, carrying stone slabs from Denny, made the first trip to Edinburgh.

The canal was a commercial venture. For twenty years, despite busy passenger and coal traffic, it struggled to pay its way. Then in 1842 the Edinburgh and Glasgow Railway was opened, trade slumped immediately and the Company faced disaster. After seven years of unequal competition they were left with little alternative but to sell out to the Railway; a decision that probably saved the canal, because the only other option would have been to abandon it. Despite closure of the Edinburgh basins in 1922 and the lock flight at Falkirk in 1933, the rest of the canal survived intact until it was closed in 1965.

A decade of madness then undid all the good fortune. Bridges were replaced by drowned culverts or pipes. New roads, most notably the M8, blocked the canal and it was buried in a mile long culvert at Wester Hailes, to make way for Edinburgh's bleak new housing scheme.

Now, the canal and many of its bridges, are listed as ancient monuments, protecting them from further ill-judged 'developments'. An expensive new aqueduct spans the Edinburgh by-pass road affirming a future for the city section, cut off by Wester Hailes. Some cut off sections, once choked by weeds and silt, have been restored to navigation. The canal's current owners, British Waterways, encourage use where possible. Boats are back on the water and life is returning to this priceless asset that our mad, rushing, 'enlightened' world, so nearly destroyed.

Great estates and farmland dominated the canal, but there were some significant towns and villages too. Ratho, once famous for its fourteen pubs, had a wide basin and wharf beside the bridge. Broxburn had cargo handling facilities at a small basin called Port Buchan. Mary Queen of Scots made Winchburgh famous when she sought refuge in nearby Niddry Castle after escaping from Loch Leven Castle in 1568. Linlithgow's neat Manse Road basin has probably got more boats in it now than in the past. The little canal museum and tea room, in a converted stables, add a new dimension to the town's 'other' heritage attractions, of the Palace and Saint Michael's Kirk. Polmont had port facilities beside Brightons Bridge, but the most important place on the whole canal was the small, unassuming village of Redding. That's where the coal mines were.

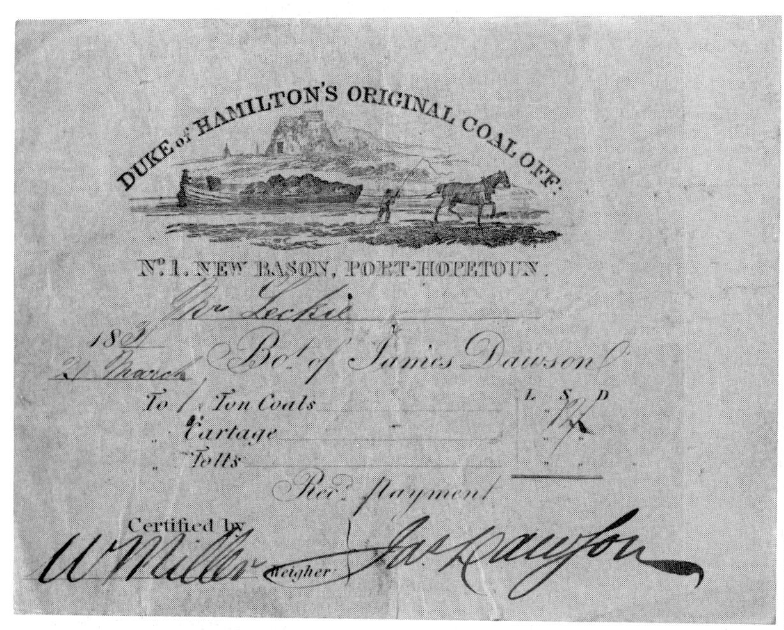

DUKE of HAMILTON'S ORIGINAL COAL OFF:

No. 1. NEW BASON, PORT-HOPETOUN.

Mr Leckie

183[illegible]
21 March

Bot. of James Dawson

	L	S	D
To 1 Ton Coals		[illegible]	
" Cartage			
" Tolls			

Recd. payment

Certified by
W Miller
Weigher
Jas Dawson

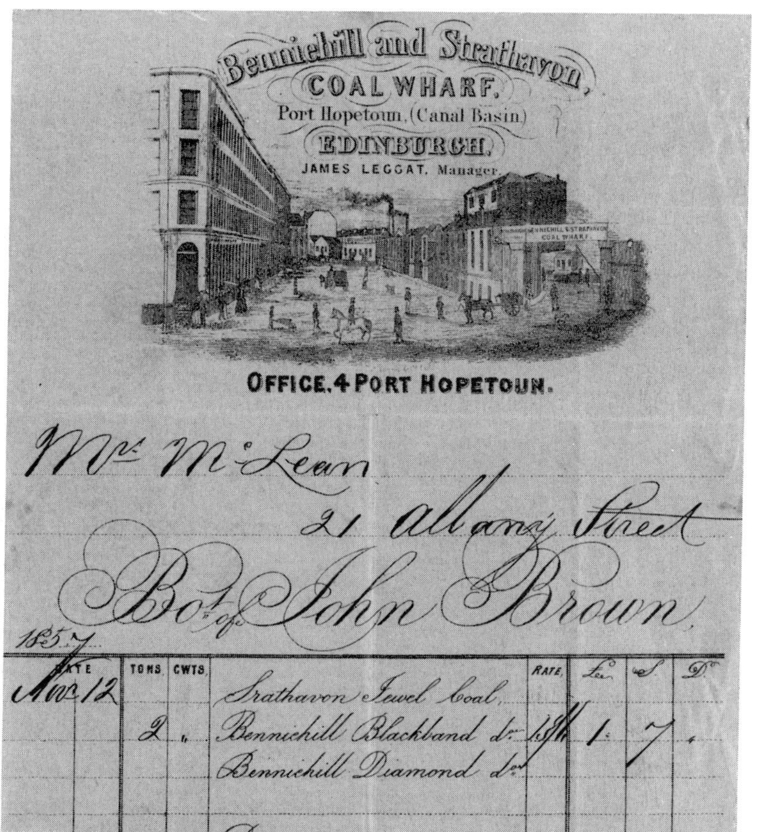

Bennichill and Strathavon,
COAL WHARF,
Port Hopetoun, (Canal Basin)
EDINBURGH,
JAMES LEGGAT, Manager.

OFFICE, 4 PORT HOPETOUN.

Mrs McLean
21 Albany Street

Bot. of John Brown

1857

Date		Tons	Cwts		Rate	£	S	D
Nov.	12			Strathavon Jewel Coal				
		2	"	Bennichill Blackband do.	[illegible]	1	7	"
				Bennichill Diamond do.				

Mineral deposits were surveyed with great care by promoters of canals and estimates of their value, as potential cargoes, formed part of their financial forecasts. As the primary reason for building the Union was to get coal into Edinburgh, surveys of coal deposits were of particular interest – no coal, no canal. The southern routes had direct access to the Monklands coalfield. So too did Baird's, but because it was a long way round through the Forth and Clyde and Monkland Canals it was important to locate a more convenience source. It was found at Redding, where, according to estimates an 'inexhaustible' supply was to be had, adjacent to the proposed canal. The Duke of Hamilton whose pits they were was, not unnaturally, an enthusiastic supporter of Baird's plan.

One of the worst pit disasters in Scotland happened at the number 23 pit at Redding on 25th September 1923. Water, which had accumulated in old adjacent mine workings, burst into the pit killing thirty seven miners. Suggestions that it was canal water were dismissed as absurd. So intense was the rush of water through the old workings that an abandoned mine shaft a mile away caved in. A mother saved her two year old girl just before the gaping hole appeared. The mine rescue was heroic. Five men were brought to safety nine days after the disaster. Efforts to find others continued day and night as miners dug their way in from abandoned workings to where the miners might be trapped and divers from the Rosyth Naval Base tried to find ways through the flooded mine. The rescue was called off when the bodies of two men were found on the 19th October. They had succumbed to the effects of black damp.

Edinburgh was at the mercy of a cartel of coal merchants who, like all monopolies, fixed high prices. They were not noted for their honesty either. Coal was sold by the cartload and by judicious spreading of the loads two carts could miraculously become three. Householders bought large, carefully mined, lumps of coal known as 'big' coal which they would then break up themselves in preference to spending less on an uncertain mixture from dubious traders. The canal changed all that. Suddenly people could be reasonably confident they were getting what they asked for at a price they could afford. This picture of a coal barge at Ratho gives a good impression of the large quantity that could be moved by canal as distinct from small horse drawn cartloads.

The Edinburgh terminal of the canal was Port Hopetoun, a single large basin beside Lothian Road. Projecting into it was this distinctive warehouse, one of the most remarkable canal buildings in Scotland. It was built to cope with increased passenger traffic. Goods traffic too became more than the port's limited facilities could handle. Coal was of course the principal cargo, but grain and building materials for the growing city were much in demand too. Stone coming in from Hailes Quarry was also re-exported through Leith to markets in England. An early indication that the opposition to Baird's plans to terminate the canal at Lothian Road, instead of Leith, may have been right. If Leith docks had been linked to the canal and through it to Glasgow, trade and the future viability of the canal might have been significantly improved.

With Port Hopetoun bursting at the seams a second basin was built to handle coal traffic. It was named Port Hamilton (the receipt on page 5 describes it as 'New Bason, Port Hopetoun') to honour the Duke of Hamilton for his prodigious efforts to provide Edinburgh with coal. He got paid as well! But while trade into Edinburgh was considerable, trade out was worryingly small. The principal export was waste. The canal gave Edinburgh the ideal solution to its problem of traffic pollution; just as big a concern for cities in the nineteenth century as it is today. But far from incurring the wrath of the surrounding countryside, farmers were only too pleased to receive the copious quantities of manure that the busy horse drawn city traffic generated. Domestic refuse also left the city by canal.

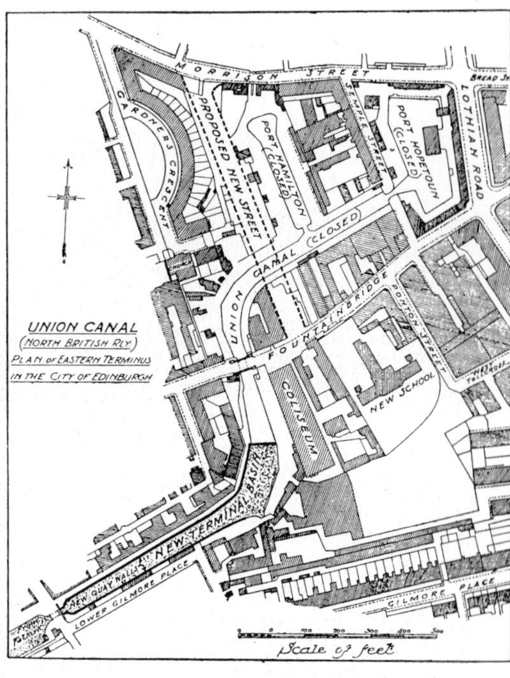

Apart from the peninsular warehouse, most of the other buildings surrounding the basins were a ramshackle collection of bothys, huts and sheds. As canal trade degenerated so did the area and by the early 1900's it had sunk to become 'one of the most hideous features of Edinburgh'. Not the sort of thing to have within a short walk of Princes Street. So, in 1922, the decayed state of the area and the insignificant volume of remaining trade persuaded the City fathers to have the basins closed. A new terminus was established on the south side of Fountainbridge. It took its name, Lochrin Basin, from an earlier basin of the same name. It was an offshoot of the main line of the canal, used by Haig's distillery and appears to have been abandoned before the 'ports'. The bricked up remains of a very low old bridge, on the offside of the 'new' Lochrin Basin, may have been the entrance to the old.

The site of Port Hopetoun at the top of Lothian Road is now occupied by Lothian House. The tax man was the first tenant, but the building is now used by a Cannon Film Centre and a variety of shops. A decorative stone carving on the front shows a barge with the inscription: 'Here stood Port Hopetoun 1822-1922'; an embarrassed, almost guilty, admission that the austere and unlovely building, opened in 1936, had replaced something much more interesting. Although this street frontage may not be very imposing, Edinburgh must now be regretting the loss of what, today, would have been a fabulous waterside amenity right in the heart of the city. An ambitious scheme, to build shops and offices around a recreated Port Hamilton was due to be completed by the end of 1991, but by that date construction hadn't even begun.

The Union is a contour canal, running for 31 miles on one level from Edinburgh to Falkirk. To achieve this, wide diversions were taken to cross the major river valleys, including a great looping curve back on itself, west of the Almond. This all added approximately six miles to the overall length. Only one flight of locks was needed, at Falkirk, to join it to the Forth and Clyde Canal, but it was necessary to construct great aqueducts and dig the first tunnel for a transport undertaking in Scotland. The level track is also characterised by long embankments and deep cuttings, like this one at Winchburgh. Despite all these works, construction was made simpler by being on the level and navigation was certainly quicker and easier.

Leaks from the embankment west of Linlithgow were always a problem and it eventually failed in the early 1980's. At the time the Union was a 'remainder waterway' with no rights of navigation and, faced with the enormous cost of repairs, British Waterways had little option but to coffer dam and de-water the breached section, approximately 500 yards. It remained like that for so long it got a name – the Kettlestoun Breach. Happily the West Lothian Canal Project, an initiative by British Waterways, the Local Authorities and the European Regional Development Fund, has now restored both the breach and the culverted Preston Road bridge, at Linlithgow, to navigation. The Linlithgow Union Canal Society can, for the first time since acquiring their little trip boat "Victoria" in 1978, sail west from Manse Road Basin to the Avon aqueduct.

The aqueducts over the River Avon near Linlithgow, the River Almond at Lin's Mill and this one over the Water of Leith at Slateford, are magnificent. The construction is so beautifully simple and elegant that photographs never do them justice. They can only really be appreciated by being there. It's hard to believe that the engineers had to divert the canal to find narrow crossing points – what' s another few hundred yards to men who could build structures like these? By the time the Union was built there were over sixty years of canal building technology behind it and these aqueducts are probably the finest expression of those skills in the British Isles. Baird based them on the Chirk and the Pontcysyllte Aqueducts on the Ellesmere Canal and consulted Thomas Telford, who had worked on the construction of both, over their design.

Of the three, the Avon is particularly awe inspiring. For maximum effect it is best viewed from below. At 810 feet long, 86 feet high and made up of 12 arches, it is the longest and tallest aqueduct in Scotland; in Britain only the Pontcysyllte is larger. The key to the success of these structures was to contain the water in an iron trough which meant that heavy stonework was not required to counter the enormous outward pressure of the water. Without the need to support a stone trough, the supporting pillars could be of a hollow, internally braced, construction giving them a more slender appearance. The deep arches that link them seem light too, despite having to take the weight of the water. The whole effect, with the trough faced with stone and topped off by iron railings is of such graceful simplicity and elegance as to belie their cold function. They were the motorway bridges of their day.

Despite being built by navvies, using only hand tools, the canal was completed in a relatively short period of time and so, like motorways today, but unlike most canals, its structures are all designed in the same style. The original plan for the Almond Aqueduct was for a single arch with embankments, but Baird changed his plans and built this, the smallest of the three 'standard' aqueducts. The skills of the men who built these great aqueducts were lost with the passing of the canal age and had to be relearned, in the 1980's, by the engineers who built the new aqueduct over the Edinburgh by-pass road at Calder Crescent. Lin's Mill, seen in this picture through the right hand arch of the Almond aqueduct, enjoys a melancholy fame as the home of William Lin, the last man to die of the plague in Scotland in 1645.

The prospect of boosting Edinburgh's inadequate water supply with fresh supplies from the canal was a significant factor in persuading the City magistrates to eventually back Baird's proposals. This might seem unsavoury today, but in the days of horse drawn boats, before oily engines stirred up the silt, canal water remained comparatively clean. There was some concern, however, about effluent from the passage (passenger) boats! Water is the life blood of any canal and the engineers had to find an ample supply to maintain the level in all weathers. Mill owners on the Almond (and the other rivers) were concerned that the canal's needs would deplete the rivers leaving insufficient flow to drive their mills. Parliament therefore, only approved plans to divert water on condition that the interests of existing users were safeguarded.

This was achieved by creating the Cobbinshaw Reservoir, ten miles from the canal in the hills above West Calder. It supplied water down the Bog Burn to 'top up' the Almond. Further downstream, just below Mid Calder, a weir (which may have been adapted from an existing mill dam) directs water out of the river and into the canal feeder. A few hundred yards after taking it out, the engineers switched the water across to the opposite bank of the river on a superb little cast iron aqueduct. After this confident flourish, the swiftly flowing stream clings to the steep sides of the river valley; a difficult construction that included four wee tunnels, a number of culverts and numerous small bridges. It is nearly three miles long and is seen here entering the canal, on the left of this unusual 'top' view of the aqueduct. The estate through which it was built is now the Almondell and Calder Wood Country Park.

Weirs, or spillways, controlled the water level by releasing the surplus into natural streams. Another simple control was to have sluices on the Slateford and Almond aqueducts which, when open, poured spectacular plumes of water into the rivers below. This was such an impressive sight that people went on special boat trips to the Almond to view it. An advertisement from the 1830's offered to '. . . entertain visitors . . . by exhibiting the Fall of Water from the Almond Viaduct (sic) into the River below . . . ' and all for just sixpence! It is still regarded as an attraction by the passengers on the restaurant boats from the Bridge Inn at Ratho. The spectacle became frozen in time as 'The Great Broxburn Icicle' in the severe winter of 1895, the subject of this perhaps most famous of all photographs of the Almond aqueduct.

The Union was never intended to take sea going boats, so the fixed stone arch bridges only had to accommodate barges and passage boats. They were built to a standard specification, so they all look similar, but not the same. There are differences in span and width and the stone parapets are varied on some bridges by iron railings. The bridge numbers are carved in the key stones of the arches. They start from bridge number 1 at Viewforth in Edinburgh to number 62, Bantaskine Bridge in Falkirk. It is the most photographed bridge on the canal, as these pictures from the early 1900's show. Watch the telegraph pole; it's not in the top picture, in the left hand picture it's waiting on the towpath to be erected and there it is, poking above the bridge, in the right hand picture. Bantaskine was a popular spot.

Inevitably bridges over cuttings were different to the others, although they usually had the same shape of arch. Not so at Glen Village, east of Falkirk where much greater arches were needed to span the deep cutting on the approach to the tunnel. One of these bridges has a laughing face carved on its eastern keystone and a very unhappy face on the west. It is known as the laughin', greetin' bridge. The popular explanation is that the laughing face represents the contractor who got rich, making the relatively easy cut to the east, while the unhappy care worn contractor to the west was bankrupted by a task made difficult by the tunnel and locks. Since these were apparently separate contracts this may not be true, but why should that ruin a good story?

Bridge number 1 also had carved keystones, with Edinburgh's coat of arms on the east side and Glasgow's on the west. Boats leaving Edinburgh for the west had to pass through three bridges before they even got to it. There was a little wooden draw-bridge in Semple Street at the entrance to Port Hopetoun, while boats leaving Port Hamilton passed under an elevated wooden footbridge. At Fountainbridge the deck of this electrically operated 'Leamington Bridge' would be raised between gantries on either side of the road to allow boats to pass. This fascinating bridge was re-sited at Gilmore Park, to replace another wooden draw-bridge, when the city basins were closed in 1922. The keeper of the original Gilmore Park bridge upset local residents in 1827, who objected to the offensive smell from his cow-shed, pig-sty and D.I.Y. abbatoir; not the sort of staff enterprise that British Waterways would encourage today!

The canal was the first purpose built 'highway' between the two cities. It was followed by the railway and then new motor roads which have been upgraded many times. This picture from the 1930's shows the bridge near Broxburn carrying the infamous ('I hate the ..') A8 road (now the A89) over the canal, with one of the original bridges behind it. The most recent upgrading of the road to motorway standard allowed one of the most stunning acts of official vandalism to be perpetrated on the Scottish canal system. A few hundred yards east of this bridge, the M8 motorway has been built on a drowned culvert, blocking the canal. This was modern engineering's unimaginative solution to the problem of the Almond Valley; a folly that will cost a lot to put right.

Today the 'green' links that canals form between town and country offer a tranquil, traffic free escape from the overwhelming intrusions of modern life. In the early nineteenth century, however, it was the canals that were regarded as the intrusion. Baird had to take great care planning the canal to avoid offending the many wealthy landowners along the route. The owner of Glenfuir House at Camelon was faced with the prospect of having the Forth and Clyde Canal to the north, the Union to the south and the lock flight joining them to the west. Compensation for this loss of amenity was resolved when he forced the Canal Company to buy the whole estate. William Forbes was so appalled at the prospect of having to look at the canal that he refused to allow it to pass within sight of his Callendar House, thus forcing the construction of the only canal tunnel in Scotland, under Prospect Hill near Falkirk.

The tunnel is 690 yards long and has a towpath running through it. It is cut out of solid rock and there are deep rock cuttings at each end. Water seeps steadily through the roof and the sound of splashing and dripping is the constant accompaniment to a walk or sail through it. Apparently a miner, walking through one night, found he had some unwelcome company. A barge had got stuck in the tunnel and the bargeman had gone off to get help. The miner, a wee bit the worse for drink, blundered into the abandoned horse which reared up in the dark giving him a terrible fright. Sobering up instantly he rushed from the tunnel, convinced his encounter had been with the Devil. Apparently he didn't touch the (Demon) drink for at least two weeks.

Falkirk can not only boast the only canal tunnel in Scotland, but also, just under a mile to the west, the only locks on the Union Canal. There were eleven; each was 69 feet long and 12 feet 6 inches wide and had a fall of 10 feet. They dropped down in a wide sweeping curve to a huge basin beside Lock 16 on the Forth and Clyde Canal. It was called Port Downie after Robert Downie of Appin, President of the Canal Company. Thomas Telford had suggested continuing the canal to join the Forth and Clyde at its summit at Wyndford Lock, three miles east of Kilsyth. So too did Robert Stevenson in his plan. This would have saved considerable time in through navigation between Glasgow and Edinburgh, because it would have cut out four locks on the Forth and Clyde and reduced the number joining the two canals together to six. But it would have meant cutting at least six more miles of canal and erecting another great aqueduct at Castlecary!

Port Downie quickly became a busy junction. Passengers travelling between the two cities were attracted in great numbers. Initially there were not enough boats and on special occasions, like the visit of King George IV to Edinburgh in 1822, barges were fitted with planks, as seats, to cope with the demand. Catering at Port Downie was also in demand and John Renkeillor, a Canal Company tenant at Lock 16, met it by supplying refreshments at his house. He did such good business that the Company was persuaded to build the Union Inn, the distinctive building between the two canals in this picture. Renkeillor was its first landlord. The picture from the turn of the century demonstrates the contrast then, between the relatively busy Forth and Clyde on the right and the empty Union.

Separate passenger services operated day and night on the two canals. Passengers had to walk almost a mile, with their luggage, to change boats at Port Downie. Not much fun in the middle of the night and especially unpleasant in winter, so the canal was extended east from the top lock by 570 yards to this new terminus called Port Maxwell. It was little more than a squared off end to the canal, but it shortened the walk considerably. The early passenger boats were simple craft, but in 1830 a wooden twin hulled boat called 'Swift' was tried out between Glasgow and Edinburgh. She completed the return journey in just over six and a half hours at speeds averaging nine miles per hour. The twin hulled boats that followed her were made of light iron and took the generic name of 'Swift'.

For the next few years these fast boats reigned supreme. Then in 1840 a railway was built from Slammannan near Airdrie to a basin at Causewayend, near the Avon Aqueduct. The Company hoped it would establish a rail/canal link between Glasgow and Edinburgh and prevent a railway being built between the two cities. It was an optimistic hope. The canal faced competition from stage coaches and was put at a disadvantage when the railway stopped selling connecting boat tickets, but continued to sell them for the coaches. Also, if the boat was late, the train would go without the canal passengers. Two years later, the Edinburgh and Glasgow Railway was open and the canal had to fight for survival. Boat speeds were cut to save horses and fares were cut to attract passengers, but to no avail. Through passenger services ceased in 1848, although a local service between Port Hopetoun and Broxburn continued for a while.

The Falkirk locks had individual side reservoirs to supply them with water, used more by bathers than boaters in later years. The railway was the main reason for this demise. It crossed the locks on this viaduct, known as Summerford Bridge (or as in this picture, 'King's Bridge'). It was made up of six arches of varying sizes. The main span 130'0" wide and 24'6" high was reputed to be the largest single stone arch of such a low elevation in Britain. The way the canal itself was engineered presaged its downfall. The level track with cuttings and embankments, maintained by the great aqueducts and tunnel and crossed by an unusually large number of bridges and underpasses, was much more like the railways that followed it than the canals that had preceded it. It was a prototype for a railway.

By the turn of the century the principal industries of the area around Port Downie were chemicals and iron founding. The North British Railway which owned the Union Canal and the Caledonian Railway which owned the Forth and Clyde competed vigorously to attract the trade from these industries away from their rivals and onto their own systems. Such was the intensity of this 'battle' that the two railway companies also competed directly with their own canals. The Union suffered most. Cut off from these potentially lucrative markets and with branch railways weaving around the locks starving them of trade, boat movements between the two canals dwindled to nothing. The locks were closed in 1933 and along with Port Downie, filled in. They had been hidden from view until recent engineering work by British Waterways revealed one of the chambers. It has been left partially exposed. The Union Inn is all that is left of Port Downie today.

A year after the withdrawal of passenger services, the railway took over the canal itself. But instead of heralding an immediate end to cargo carrying, the railway, bound by an Act of Parliament to maintain the canal in working order, had an incentive to encourage it. Nevertheless, goods carrying did decline and in the early years of the twentieth century dwindled rapidly. In 1905 56 boats carried 100,000 tons, in 1913 40 boats moved 65,000 tons and by 1921 there were only 32 boats on the canal carrying a mere 20,000 tons. This picture from the early 1950's shows one of only a few work boats left on the canal. The boat is being towed by a man – 'bow hauled', a not uncommon way to move short haul boats on canals, yet somehow symbolic of the last sad years of commercial decline. The towpath too has shrunk to a narrow track.

There were boatbuilding yards, here at Causewayend, where there was also a dry dock, and in Edinburgh at Port Hopetoun and Gilmore Place. Boats were also built at Leith and at the Tophill yard at Falkirk on the Forth and Clyde Canal. Barges on Central Scotland's canals came in two sizes. The big boats pulled by two horses were called lighters while the smaller ones, those used on the Union, were called scows. Scow is an old Scots word meaning flat bottomed boat. Until recently, there were few powered boats on the Union. A screw propelled steam 'swift' was tried out in 1840 and a steam passage boat the 'Edinburgh' lasted only three months before she collided with a bridge at night and was withdrawn. More recently, in 1959, British Waterways experimented with two hire cruisers, a far sighted initiative that sadly failed.

Few industries were attracted to the canal. Some, however, like the North British Rubber Works here at Lochrin Basin and distilleries in Edinburgh and Linlithgow drew water supplies from it. This not only provided valuable revenue but also saved the canal from being filled in. Of the other industries, there was an iron works at the Causewayend trans-shipment basin as well as that ill-fated railway terminal. The basin is unusual, square with high sides and has the general appearance of a tidal dock. Nobel's factory at Redding made explosives, vitriol, detonators and other chemicals. The Winchburgh brick works was the last commercial user of the canal. It stopped sending barge loads of bricks into Edinburgh in 1937 when the aqueduct over Slateford Road was closed for reconstruction. The bricks were made from spent shale.

The most dramatic example of the canal's failure to attract industry was the scant use made of it by the shale oil industry. The enormous bings that dominate the West Lothian landscape are testimony to the scale of this once thriving industry. The tragedy for the canal is that some of the biggest oil works at Philipstoun, Winchburgh and here at Broxburn were right beside the canal; yet they scarcely used it. Their legacy, the bings, perhaps contribute more now to the canal, in heritage value, than the living industry ever did. Shale oil's place amongst the country's great industries is curiously undervalued, because the man who started it, James 'Parrafin' Young, is regarded as the world's first oil man (eat your heart out J.R.). He created an industry that lasted for over a hundred years and employed thousands of people in over a hundred works and associated industries. And yet, you will have to look hard to find any statue or memorial to him.

Young began his career by producing oils, from a natural spring of naptha found in a Derbyshire coal mine. When that dried up he returned to Scotland and began to experiment with producing oil from coal. He set up his first oil works at Bathgate in 1850 (ten years before the first American 'gusher') using 'Cannel' (candle) coal, or Torbanite which gave a good yield of parrafin when roasted or 'retorted'. The supply of Torbanite was quickly exhausted and Young's search for an alternative mineral led him to the abundant deposits of shale to be found in West Lothian. The seams of shale occurred at various depths sometimes dipping at considerable angles as shown by this picture of a Broxburn mine. When the shale had been extracted, the mine roof was allowed to collpase, so where deposits were close to the surface, seams had to be left intact under roads, houses, or the canal, to prevent subsidence.

It took a ton of good quality shale to produce forty gallons of oil, but in later years poorer shale only yielded eighteen gallons. Sixteen hundredweight of spent shale was left, to swell the huge, unsightly, red bings. The oil works that spawned them were none too pretty either. But their products were in widespread and everyday use; candles, lighthouse oil, sulphate of ammonia, a variety of lubricants, fuel oils, diesel, petrol – Ross's Petrol produced at these Phillipstoun works of James Ross and Co. and of course parafin. Scottish parrafin had a higher flashpoint and was vastly superior to the cheap American imitations that caused so much fire damage (and delighted Western movie makers). The whole West Lothian industry was bought out in 1919 by the Anglo Persian Oil Company, the forerunner of B.P. It remained as part of B.P., called Scottish Oils, until its closure in 1962.

The most significant discovery associated with the canal itself, was the observance in 1834 of the solitary wave phenomenon, or 'soliton', by John Scott Russell. He was watching experiments with boat haulage at Hermiston when he noticed that the wave, built up in front of the boat, carried on at the same speed when the boat stopped suddenly. He followed the wave on horseback for up to two miles before he lost sight of it. This discovery influenced his later work on naval architecture which included Isambard Kingdom Brunel's 'Great Eastern'. It was still being evaluated by designers of racing yachts in the 1960's and is now set to revolutionise the electronics industry. The soliton is clearly a wave that will run and run, be it in water or down a fibre optic. This was not an isolated association with the canal for Scott-Russell. He also designed a headlamp for the night boats which without proper illumination risked serious accidents travelling at speed in the dark.

Navigators, navvies, men who built canals, or 'navigations', came in huge numbers from all over the British Isles to work on the Union. Local communities dreaded their arrival and feared their presence. Irish navvies were preferred to Highlanders who tended to 'disappear' at harvest time. Two Irish navvies who continued to work on the canal after it was finished were William Hare and William Burke – Burke and Hare. Hare worked as a docker at Port Hopetoun. He also acted as a porter and 'assisted' passengers with their luggage to lodgings at Tanner's Close, about three hundred yards away. Some never returned. The canal not only brought the two murderers together, but gave them, and other body snatchers like them, the opportunity to range far and wide in their search for fresh bodies. Graveyards at canalside churches like Muiravonside would have been easy to raid, the spoils transported by boat to the anatomy classes in Edinburgh.

Many former navvies, like Burke, became maintenance men, or 'banksmen'. This picture, taken between 1884 and 1890, shows a group of pipe smoking banksmen at Wilkie's Basin, west of Ratho. They looked after the stretch of canal near the basin, supervised by John Tait, the man on the right. The old man in the centre of the group looks more like a 'baccy spittin' ole' cowpoke on a Wild West lynching mob than a Scottish canal man. He could have been old enough to have witnessed the construction of the canal, or even worked on it as a boy! The men's clothing, the way it is patched, held together by string and with nails or matches for buttons, graphically illustrates their social status. But the string round their ankles and knees has more to do with a desire to stop rats running up their trouser legs than any concession to poverty.

Banksmen would inspect the canal for leaks early in the morning, when the world was still and quiet. The slightest sound or disturbance in the water would indicate a problem. Leaks from embankments on hillsides, like this one at Bantaskine, had to be detected early to prevent breaching and collapse of the canal bed, as at Kettlestoun. Clearing rubbish was necessary too. The men here, with the bank boat 'Francis', seem to be removing weed and other 'natural' rubbish, but in the city all sorts of junk was discarded in the canal. So, because no boats moved on New Year's Day, the water was drained and the maintenance men cured their Hogmanay hangover by hauling it all back out again. Not an ideal way to celebrate, but no doubt the occasional passing well wisher would offer some liquid compensation. ". . . I don't . . . that is . . . not while I'm . . . well, if you insist . . . and a Guid New Year to you too sir!"

This funny looking boat, like a floating steel slug, in the Causewayend dry dock, was the ice breaker. Ice was always a problem on canals particularly for wooden hulled boats and so ice breakers were needed to keep the channel free. The action of rocking the boat from side to side was one way of breaking up the ice. The other was to haul the boat up on to the ice which would give way under its weight. In really severe weather there was simply no way of keeping the channel free. Detractors were quick to seize on the canals' discomfort in the severe winter of 1838, when nothing moved for two months. The freeze up of February 1895 not only created the Broxburn Icicle but also a foot of ice on the canal. Too much for a steel slug to cope with!

If ice was the problem in winter, the problem in summer was weed and this weed cutter was used in the 1930's to keep this perennial problem under control. With shallow water and few boat movements, the canal was prone to weeding up. A major problem for canals in predominantly agricultural countryside, like the Union, is that fertilisers leech off fields into the water and stimulate a healthy weed growth. The fertility of canalside fields, encouraged originally by Edinburgh's manure, has in more recent times near Ratho, yielded world record crops of wheat grown per acre. Some farmers apparently used their own scows to take fresh produce quickly to the markets. Whether they returned with manure in the same boat (gulp!) is not known.

As the numbers of commercial craft dwindled, the numbers of rowing boats, canoes and other small craft increased. Pictures from Edwardian times up to the 1930's and 40's show that leisure boating was a popular pastime, particularly at Falkirk. Boats were available at Bantaskine Bridge and here at the boating station beside the top lock. The canal, from the tunnel, through Bantaskine to the locks and Port Maxwell, was also a favourite haunt of young lovers. As if to emphasise the attraction, some picture postcards of Edwardian days describe it as 'lovers' walk'. Couples could stroll along the towpath hand in hand or hire a boat and row to some secluded spot, with only the ducks, swans and dozens of other people rowing to secluded spots to disturb them.

In Edinburgh, rowing boats and canoes could be hired at Slateford, where they could be rowed out into the countryside at Hermiston. Boats could also be hired close to the city centre at Johnston's boathouses, here beside Lochrin Basin, an activity that has now been revived by the Edinburgh Canal Society from its Harrison Park boathouse. Elsewhere boats can now be hired at Ratho and Linlithgow. The Forth Canoe Club has slung slalom poles across Lochrin Basin to practice canoeing, which is popular at all levels, on the canal. Punting has been introduced by the Honourable Society of Edinburgh Boaters. Their highly uncompetitive races usually end in their defeat, with somebody falling overboard and a further soaking in the pub!

Serious rowing is also popular in Edinburgh. Rowing technique can be observed and perfected from the tow path, because it is so close to the boat. Saint Andrew's Boat Club at Meggetland is the oldest established club on the canal, dating from 1846. It is open to all-comers. Edinburgh University and the big Edinburgh schools, George Watson's, George Heriot's and Stewart Melville's also use the canal for rowing. The canal is too narrow for boats to race side by side, so they have 'station' races. The boats start with one three lengths in front of the other. There are two finishing posts and if one boat has extended or closed the gap on the other, it is the winner. The pictures show St. Andrew's University being beaten by Glasgow University at the Edinburgh University Regatta in 1924. Glasgow is the boat on the left of the lower picture.

It is somehow fitting of a prim canal like the Union that the fondest memories people have of it are of going on a Sunday School trip. Barges were scrubbed clean for the occasion and fitted with planks for seats (just like the 'old days'). Pictures show boats and barges loaded (overloaded by today's regulated standards) with young people who seem happy and excited, despite the overcrowding and lack of creature comforts. These were days full of care-free fun and gaiety with sack races, egg and spoon races, three legged races and of course picnics in the sunshine – the sun always shone! The trips from Edinburgh went to a field near Ratho and those from Linlithgow, like this small boat, went to Philipstoun, but such was the popularity of these trips, that there must have been many destinations all along the canal.

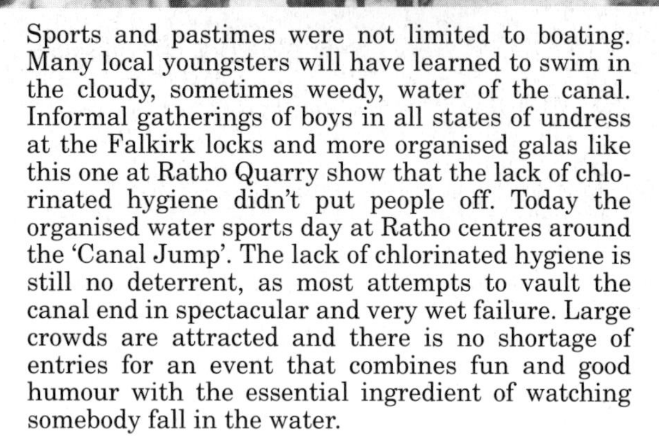

Sports and pastimes were not limited to boating. Many local youngsters will have learned to swim in the cloudy, sometimes weedy, water of the canal. Informal gatherings of boys in all states of undress at the Falkirk locks and more organised galas like this one at Ratho Quarry show that the lack of chlorinated hygiene didn't put people off. Today the organised water sports day at Ratho centres around the 'Canal Jump'. The lack of chlorinated hygiene is still no deterrent, as most attempts to vault the canal end in spectacular and very wet failure. Large crowds are attracted and there is no shortage of entries for an event that combines fun and good humour with the essential ingredient of watching somebody fall in the water.

The old stables building at Woodcockdale, west of Linlithgow, was used in the 1830's by the horses on the fast passenger boats. It had a dwelling house at each end and a stables in the centre. When the house at the east end became vacant in 1942 a new Sea Scout Troop, the 1st West Lothian, was formed to occupy it. Apart from a recent difficulty with the lease, they have been there ever since, taking over the whole building as the other tenants and British Waterways moved out. A Sea Scout troop on a canal, only four miles from the sea, may seem odd, but apparently the sea is not essential for their activities, only water. They have made full use of it, learning canoeing and other boat handling skills. The Sea Scouts must now be one of the longest continuing users of the canal in its history and their efforts have ensured the survival of one of the few remaining original buildings.

The first canal marathon for inflatable boats in 1974 left Edinburgh and finished the next day with a (boat ripping) last lap down the River Kelvin to Kelvingrove Park in Glasgow. By 1978 the race was organised by the Linlithgow Union Canal Society, sponsored by The Drambuie Liqueur Company, stayed on the canals and went from Glasgow to Edinburgh. Being a veteran of these madcap enterprises, I will resist the temptation to bore you with exaggerated tales of derring-do and confine myself to telling you that my trusty partner Donald MacKinnon (alas, no relation to the MacKinnons of Drambuie) and I, won the event in 1984 and 1985 and 'we was robbed' of the hat-trick by a burst boat in 1986. The pictures show the 'Ton-up Kids' (the nick name we acquired for being old enough to know better) in action on the Union.

Big boats, too, returned to the canal in 1974, when the 'Pride of the Union' arrived on a lorry from her builders in Birmingham. She was lowered into the water at Wilkie's Basin to begin her maiden trip to the Bridge Inn at Ratho. It was plagued by difficulties, but she made it to become the first canal restaurant boat in Scotland and set a pioneering trend. The Linlithgow Union Canal Society added to the activity in 1978 with the launch at Manse Road Basin of their delightful replica of a 19th century steam packet 'Victoria'. Ratho also became the base for the Seagull Trust, a charity that promotes canal cruising for disabled people. The 'Saint John Crusader' was their first boat, launched in 1979, followed by the 'MacKay Seagull'. 'Janet Telford', now at Linlithgow, joined them and the 'Govan Seagull' built by apprentices at Govan Shipbuilders operates from a new boathouse at Bantaskine. The Union Canal has come back to life.

SELECT BIBLIOGRAPHY

Jean Lindsay	The Canals of Scotland, pub: David and Charles, 1968
E.A. Pratt	Scottish Canals and Waterways, pub: Selwyn and Blount 1922
Basil Skinner	The Union Canal, pub: Linlithgow Union Canal Society 1977 and 1990
Alison Massey	The Edinburgh and Glasgow Union Canal, pub: Falkirk Museums, 1983
British Waterways	three pamphlets: Union Canal, Fountainbridge to Wester Hailes, 1987; Wester Hailes to the M8, 1988; The M8 to the Avon Aqueduct, 1991.
A.I. (Ian) Bowman	Swifts and Queens, pub: Strathkelvin District Libraries and Museums, 1984
Don Martin and A.A. MacLean	Edinburgh and Glasgow Railway Guidebook, pub: Strathkelvin District Libraries and Museums, 1992
M. J. Worling	Early Railways of the Lothians, pub: Midlothian District Libraries, 1991
Paul Carter (Editor)	The Forth and Clyde Canal Guidebook, pub: Strathkelvin District Libraries and Museum, 1991.
Linlithgow Union Canal Society	A Companion for Canal Passengers betwixt Edinburgh and Glasgow 1823; reprinted 1981.

ACKNOWLEDGEMENTS

I am grateful for permission to use the remarkable photographs on the front cover and pages 8, 9, 10, 11, 22 and 45. They are from the Chrystal collection; Copyright: Royal Commission on the Ancient and Historical Monuments of Scotland.

I am grateful also to Ronnie Rusack of the Bridge Inn at Ratho for his help, encouragement and permission to use pictures on pages 7, 40, 43, 47 and 48. Judy Gray of the Linlithgow Union Canal Society was a tremendous help and I am indebted to her and the Society for permission to use pictures on pages 17 and 33. Judy and Ronnie also introduced me to the pictures of M.G.C.W. (Michael) Wheeler. Taken in the 1950's and 1970's they are now almost as priceless an archive as the wonderful Chrystal collection. I am grateful to Michael for permission to use pictures on pages 32, 34 and 42. Helen Rowbotham of British Waterways has amassed a fund of knowledge about the canal and her cheerful help and advice was invaluable. The superb display on the shale oil industry at the Almond Valley Heritage Centre at Livingstone is worth a visit and I am grateful to Dr. Robin Chesters, of the Centre, for permission to use the picture on page 37. I must also thank John MacDonald for the picture on page 49, Margaret Graham for permission to use the picture on page 36, Bob McCutcheon for the pictures on pages 1 and 44, and Dougie Johnstone, whose photographs from more recent times will also form a valuable future archive, for the pictures on pages 50 and 51.

I must also thank; Malcolm Cant for his kindness and help, Stanley Ross Smith of the Scottish Inland Waterways Association, George Hunter of the Scottish Amateur Rowing Association, the staff of the Almondell and Calder Wood Country Park, Don Martin of Strathkelvin District Libraries and Alan Currie of British Waterways, for his local knowledge.

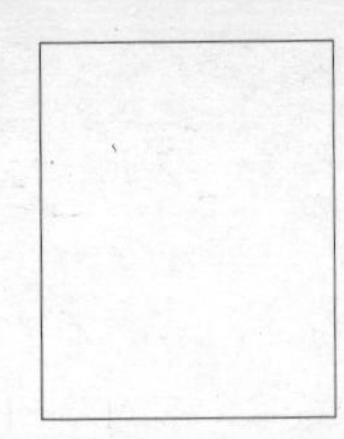

Gromit hears a lorry brake sharply at the lights on 62 West Wallaby Street.

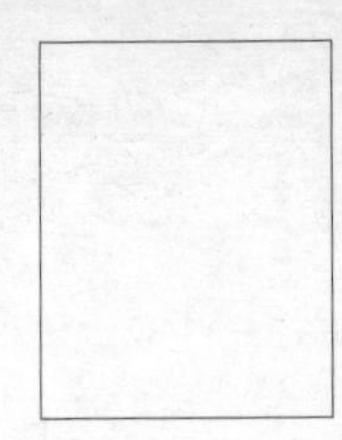

The lamb jumped out of the lorry
and ran into No. 62...

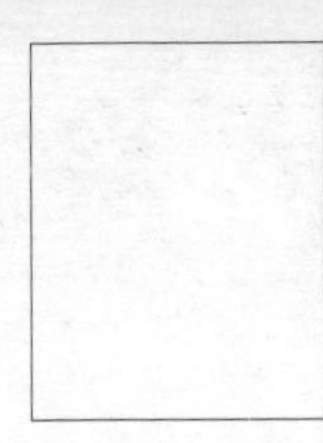

Wallace stopped smiling as the porridge cannon went on firing.

"Er, *mice*, d'you think, Gromit?"

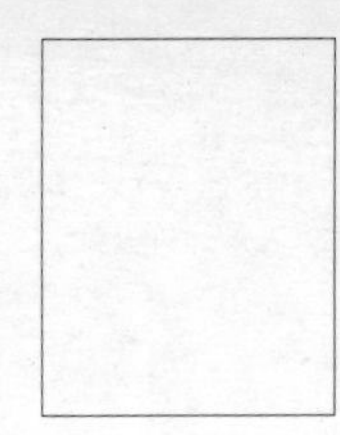

"Gromit, you know we're doing the clock tomorrow?"

Approaching *Wendolene's Wools*.

WAL 1
GO

The *Wash'n'Go* window cleaners
roared out of the garage.

WAL 1

Wallace braked hard and sent Gromit pole-vaulting into the air.

Wools
WOOL-EWE-LIKE

Right on time Wallace handed over the bucket and sponge.

WOOL
RATIONING
TWO BALLS
PER
PERSON

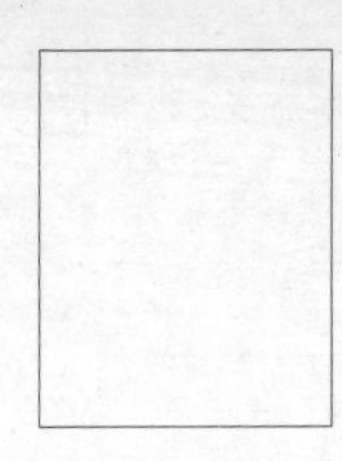

"It's my oppo, you see... does a bit of knitting."

From *A Close Shave*

Gromit was shocked to see they were
holding hands!

"Your dog's waiting..."

From *A Close Shave*

The kitchen was a mess and the culprit was stuck in some treacle.

Gromit programmed the machine
to wash the lamb.

"What I need is a good sheepdog!"

Gromit looked at his gift - what a cruel joke!